My L

from my

Experiences

Seven Keys to turn
Trials into Triumphs

Benny King

Unless otherwise indicated, all scripture quotations are taken from the King James Version of the Bible.

My Lessons *from my* Experiences
Seven Keys to turn Trials into Triumphs
Benny King

ISBN: 0-9543301

FOR WORLD WIDE DISTRIBUTION
Published by Crown Gospel Inc. London

Designed & Printed by Divine Connections
London

CONTENTS

FOREWORD BY DR MYLES MUNROE

The desire to achieve and succeed is inherent in the heart of all humans, no matter their socio-economic status.
However, only a small percentage of the world's population will experience the level of success desired.

This lack of personal achievement is due in some cases to lack of opportunity, disadvantaged situations and limited external resources.

However, in the majority of cases, many people fail to achieve their God-given purpose and potential due to their ignorance of or failure to effectively apply the eternal principles and laws of life established by God the Creator.

Life was designed for success and created for you and I to achieve and experience God's destiny and vision for our lives. However, life was also designed to function according to set laws and principles that guarantee success.

If we learn and apply these laws as laid down by the Creator of life, success will be inevitable and would take us from being victims to experiencing the joy of victory.

Benny King, in ‘My Lessons From My Experiences’ breaks these fundamental principles down for us all to apply and through his personal experience and achievements, he makes them simple and practical.

In his direct approach, Benny leaps over complicated formulas and theories to represent these vital principles from the source of all wisdom: the Bible.

‘My Lessons From My Experiences’ shows us that no matter where we are, regardless what situation we may find ourselves in and irrespective what our social or economic condition may be, if we follow these time-tested laws of success, we can make that vertical leap to the place of success designed for each of us by God.

Benny’s personal testimony and living example is evidence that what he writes is proven and true.

I admonish you to peal the wisdom and insights from these pages and through diligent application and commitment, watch your life also make that vertical leap.

Dr Myles Munroe,
Nassau,
The Bahamas.

ACKNOWLEDGEMENTS

I would like to express my deep gratitude to a few people whose support has been pivotal for the successful writing and publication of this book.

Firstly, I would like to thank my wife Tayo for her unstinting support and unwavering belief in me, not to mention her words of encouragement, which gave me the inspiration to move on from each chapter of this book to the next.

I would like to thank my pastor Rev. Matthew Ashimolowo who knew what message I carried in me.

Pastor, yours was the counsel that steered me towards writing this book when it might have been easier for me to write on something else that would never have been truly representative of what God was calling me to write about first.

Many thanks also to my spiritual father Dr Myles Munroe who despite his busy schedule so willingly made himself available to give the support, guidance and encouragement necessary for the completion of this book.

Pops, it was your messages during the Winning Ways crusades in Ghana in March 2001 that gave me the self confidence which spurred me to continue with this book at times when I was so tempted to give up.

A special mention as well to my friend Jenny Joseph who weathered all the stormier periods of our friendship and never let me forget that there was a writer in me.

Without this invaluable friendship, I would have closed the writing chapter of my life and neither this nor any of the other books I will write in the future would have ever seen the light of day. And strange as it may sound, I would also like to thank all those people who have imposed severe persecution and ill treatment on me.

Without their provocation, it would have been very easy for me to stay in the comfort zone, when there was so much II could do on my own, using the talent that God has richly blessed me with, for the edification of the body of Christ.

Finally, I would like to thank God the Father of my Lord and Saviour Jesus Christ who picked up this broken vessel and saw fit to use it in such a way so as to bring glory to His Name.

DEDICATION

"Arise, shine; for your light has come! And the glory of the Lord is risen upon you.
For behold, the darkness shall cover the earth, and deep darkness the people; But the Lord will arise over you, and His glory will be seen upon you."
(Isaiah 60 vs. 1-2)

This book is dedicated to every reader and to everyone whose life God will change through the various projects and visions, which He has planted in me.

One thing I have always prayed for is that I should be an example of the things, which I have shared in the various arms of my ministry.

This book was written at a time of great difficulty and I have a firm conviction that without the adversity, the pressure to write the book would not have been as great.

As such, the people whose lives will be changed by this book might have had to wait much longer before it was written and printed.

The one example above all else, which I would like this to serve as, is that if I could write this book despite the hardships I was going through, then you the reader to whom it is dedicated must also spring into action.

A period of adversity must be used to take stock of yourself, ask yourself what gifts you have and what you could do with them; This is not a time to feel sad or angry about what you are going through. It's the time to do the things that you wouldn't have done otherwise.

Sometimes, we let our hearts become so crowded with various feelings, that they become the distractions which leave us with too little time to think about anything more productive - like how we can best use the gifts that still lie buried and untapped within us.

If this book drives you to rise out of the dust of anger and discouragement and you begin to do something more productive and meaningful with your life like re-discovering your purpose and re-identifying your potential and acting on both then it would have been worth writing.

The vision for this book is borne out in the scripture at the top of this chapter : it is designed to cause you to rise and begin to shine in the way that God intended when He created you; the glory of the Lord is indeed risen upon you; the time has come for the rest of us to see it.

PREFACE

"The Lord our God spoke to us in Horeb, saying: 'You have dwelt long enough at this mountain. Turn and take your journey…."
(Deuteronomy 1 vs. 6 - 7a)

Many years ago, in the heat of an argument, someone spoke the following words in my ears :"You're nothing but a born loser and a no-hoper and a waste of space ! "

No language has a vocabulary wide enough to adequately describe just how deeply those words cut to the very depth of my being.

But the greatest damage done was not that the words were spoken, it was in the decision, which I made and followed through, for many years after.

You see, I could have done one of two things; I could have dismissed them as the lies that they were, or I could have believed them.
I chose to believe they were true and I let them govern the way I saw myself in the years that followed.

No-one could have convinced me that today, so many years after I heard those devastating words, I would be writing a book to help people whose lives have been torn apart by words, experiences, events and all the other things which we have allowed to shape our minds, and consequently our lives.

Today, you may think that the place of hardship, which you currently occupy, is the result of something someone said, or maybe even something that happened to you, but I came to let you know that where you are now does not have to be your final destination.

When someone called me a born loser, a no-hoper and a waste of space all those years ago, I sank as low as I could, and I stayed at rock bottom.

And then every rejection I suffered afterwards was interpreted in my mind as proof that those words were indeed true.

But my rise out of that pit was not because someone somewhere gave me a break.

It was because I made a decision that - having dwelt long enough on the mountain of self-rejection - it was time to move on and take steps towards the promised land that God had prepared for me even before I was born.

Whatever events got you where you are right now have passed, but their greatest effect in your life is not that they happened, it is that you continue to allow them to dominate your thinking and your life.

God loves you too much to let your entire life be determined by words spoken by people or the events you have experienced.

Everything you need in order to begin to move on from where you are has already been placed on the inside of you and from here on, you can make it.

"Blessed be the God and Father of our Lord Jesus Christ, the Father of mercies and God of all comfort, who comforts us in all our tribulation, that we may be able to comfort those who are in any trouble with the comfort with which we ourselves are comforted by God."
2 Cor. 1 vs. 3 – 4

Some day in the future, you will encourage someone to make a better go of their life than they already have and what will give everything you say the authenticity to make that person believe you is the experiences or words that got you where you are.

The only people who have the ability to encourage others to succeed in spite of past events are the ones who made it in spite of past events.

Had I not heard those terrible words, or suffered some of the other experiences, which I will share with you in the coming chapters, this book would never have been written.

'My Lessons From My Experiences' is a combination of scriptures, stories of some of the experiences I have been through and some keys I followed.

These are keys that will enable you to begin to transform your life from where you are to where God is taking you; they worked for me and I am sure they will work for you too.

It is my hope that as I came through some of my own personal experiences to write this book, you too will begin to recognise that there are projects and great successes that are waiting for you on the other side of what you are going through right now.

And when your life changes, please do not forget to do two things:

A. Thank God for what He has done to change your life, and for the gifts He had equipped you with for the successes you are currently and will always enjoy.

B. Tell someone else what you went through and

how you made it, so that they too can experience the kind of transformation which you are about to experience from this day forward.

It moves God to help you make it through, when He knows that at the end of the day, His Name will be glorified in your life and that you will strive to use your successes to be a blessing to others.

Too often in the body of Christ, we cause people to think that in order to be a blessing, they must give money, but in fact there are times when giving someone money is not a blessing but a curse.

It is the difference between giving a man fish or teaching him how to fish.

It is the difference between encouraging dependence and helping towards independence.

The greatest blessing that you can be, after today, is not the material things you will be in a position to give others, it will be in the things you teach others that will enable them to make a success out of their lives, with material benefits following.

This book is not designed to put money in your hand; it is designed to help you to become the kind of person that money pursues.

THE AUTHOR'S EXPERIENCES

Benny King was born in 1960, the youngest of his father's 14 children.

Although he was born in London, Benny grew up in Nigeria where he was raised in Lagos by his mother.

This is his story.

"My father was the Minister of Finance in Nigeria's first civil government. With his government duties and the fact that he had 13 other children by different mothers to look after, I didn't get to see very much of him before he was killed in the military coup which subsequently led to the Nigerian civil war.

Consequently for much of my childhood, I was raised by my mother who was more or less a single and working parent with two children.

When she went to work in those days when I was not even five years old, she left me with this young man who was supposed to be looking after me and that was where a lot of my problems began.

He was clearly a disturbed youth himself with something of an evil streak running through him and as the defenceless little boy that I was,

I became the channel through which he gave expression to what he had in him.

Almost everyday, for the most trivial of things, he would drag me into my mother's bedroom, strip my shorts off and thrash me, using my mother's slippers, for what seemed like an eternity.

And even though people outside could hear my cries they never knew where I was and therefore couldn't help.

The beatings only stopped one day when my mother unexpectedly came home early one day and caught him administering yet another thrashing and decided to give him a taste of his medicine.

In 1967, we moved homes to a government-owned flat in another part of Lagos and that was where I saw more of the evil he had in him.

Aside from the daily beatings, which had now resumed, he put me through a series of ordeals, which I only survived because God had ordained that my life was not going to be cut short before I'd even begun to live it properly.

In the mornings in those days, he would run the bath and because he'd identified my love for water and frolicking around in it, he would invite me to swim in it with him.

Then suddenly, when my guard was down and I was totally relaxed, he would grab my head and shove it under the water and hold it down again for what seemed like forever.

Given that he was not even into his teens and couldn't have known how much I could last under water without air, the law of averages said he should have got it wrong and held me down too long at least once and that's all it would have taken for me to have drowned.

In addition to the beatings this time with his belts, it didn't take long before I was totally broken and ready to do just about anything he demanded, just to escape his rage.

Once he got me to that stage, the full extent of his depravity emerged.

He would take me to the toilets where I was forced to hold and lick his faeces or face either a beating there and then or another water baptism the next morning.

With these experiences, my school performances soon suffered.

In a society where your relationship with your

parents often depended on how well you did at school, coming home with poor report cards didn't exactly endear me to my mother who thought I was simply not working hard enough.

That meant many beatings at her hands as well.

Eventually, I left home and went to boarding school, rejoicing that at last, I was free.
But before long, a new menace presented itself.

In my second year, I found out I had a cousin at the school who was in the fourth form and who immediately arranged for me to be in his room where he took me under his wing.

Initially, it was great to have this older brother type figure, but I soon began to wish I'd never met him.

With my academic performances still very poor, he too decided he'd try and beat better results out of me and his favourite whip was the electric cord from a disused iron.

In those days, in boarding school, we had prep, which was a two-hour study period between 7pm and 9pm in the dining hall.

But fourth form students upwards didn't have to study in the dining hall with the rest of us and they didn't have to go to bed at 9pm.

That meant they studied in their class rooms and could stay up till the early hours if they wanted to, which many of them - my cousin included - did.

Because of his dissatisfaction with my schoolwork, he decided the prep in the dining hall was no good and made me study with him along with his classmates.

And for these study periods, I had to have my latest poor report card right in front of me as a reminder of why I was there and this was supposed to motivate me to study harder.......when I COULD study !!!

But much of the time I was up there with these older students, study was something I never got much of a chance to do.

You see, it was not the normal thing for me to be there in the class room with them, so when they came in and saw me there they'd ask why, they'd then be shown my report card and then more beatings and punishments followed.

Sometimes, after they got through beating me black and blue, I'd be forced to kneel in a corner facing the wall with my arms raised up, all night until they decided to go to bed, then I'd be released to go to bed too.

Were they really trying to help me study better?

Not really.

Because of my father's name and fame, I was perceived as someone from a wealthier background than many of them and so much of what I went through those nights when my class mates were safely tucked in their beds was fuelled more by jealousy than any desire to help me to do better at my school work.

When I did manage to stay at my seat to study, what I was frequently reminded to look at was this report card that said I was no good.

By the time I went to bed sometimes at 4am in the morning, all I could see when my eyes were shut was this document that said I was no good.

When you look at that for long enough you do soon begin to believe it, even if it isn't true.

With these kinds of experiences, things went from bad to worse and I'd go home at the end of the term with another bad report and my mother would be waiting for me with her brand of measures designed to frighten me so much I wouldn't dare fail again.
All the beatings I endured did not work to increase my schoolwork.

Eventually, in 1974 after I failed my final exams and had to repeat the class, my mother decided she was the only person who could handle to rebel I was becoming and so I was taken out of boarding school and transferred to a day school.

This also meant having to go to church most evenings to be prayed for, along with all the other children who weren't doing well at school either.

We would kneel there while all these so-called prayer warriors tried to cast the spirits of forgetfulness out of us.

Even if you didn't have any such spirits hovering around you, you certainly left there thinking they were inside and all over you, by the time these guys finished with you.

I left secondary school in 1978 after taking my O' Levels and travelled to the UK to continue my studies at a sixth form college in Oxford.

After initial successes, it wasn't long before the failures began again as I failed my A' Levels in 1980 and had to retake them this time at a tutorial institution in London.

I managed to pass, but with my grades I only managed to get into a university

Which - rightly or wrongly - had a reputation for only admitting students who were failures.

So I walked through its gates in 1981 feeling like a failure among failures.

Two and a half years later in the Summer of 1983, I graduated with a degree in International Relations.

The next stage should have been to take a Masters degree and then go back to Nigeria, but as I didn't want that and didn't feel ready to stand up to my parents, I bought more time by asking to go to another university to read Law.

As this was what my mother had always wanted me to do, she readily agreed.

But two years into the course, I failed and had to leave and enter the world of work.
At around the same time, I met the woman who was to be my first wife.

By the time we were ready to get married, I started to feel this wasn't what I wanted as I was secretly in love with someone else, but didn't know how to get out of it.

Two weeks before the wedding, I confessed my feelings to the pastor at the church I was attending.

His advice was that if I didn't go through with the wedding, it would be hard for any other woman in the church to commit herself to me, having seen me let one down already.

As I never envisaged leaving that particular church at that time, I couldn't imagine never being able to get married and duly decided to accept his advice to soldier on.

It was a disaster almost from the beginning.

When you go into a marriage secretly harbouring a deep love in your heart for someone else, those feelings never go away and before long they soon come back to haunt you.

Eight years and two children later, the marriage ended in divorce and I left home feeling I'd failed at just about everything.

In the meantime shortly after my wedding I got a job as a junior reporter with a local free newspaper.

That ended in the sack after eight months following a mix-up over holidays.

I moved on to my next job as a regional correspondent with another newspaper, thinking this was at last my dream job.

The dream soon became a nightmare.

The paper suffered as a result of the Wall Street crash of the late eighties and soon brought in this hatchet man to slash the staff down as much as he could.

One day, I received a call from him about a cheque which the company had given me, but which I had lost and not cashed.

They stopped it, they gave me a replacement and asked me to destroy the other cheque if I ever found it.

Now here was Mr Hatchet-man on the phone accusing me of having cashed the cheque, which of course I hadn't.

A few weeks later as I was clearing my office of all the old junk that needed throwing away, I came across this same cheque, which was supposed to have been cashed, and I was straight on the phone back to him.

His reply was "…leave it with me…"

As I put the phone down something told me; "King, your days are numbered.
The cheque was never cashed, he was just looking for an excuse to sack you."

When he found none over the next couple of months, he wrote me to tell me that the company could no longer afford to keep me on and was therefore making me redundant.

It's quite funny really because a few months later, he began an affair with the boss' secretary and between them, they made off with most of the company's money.

Out of that job I began making overtures into radio and travelled to London in 1988 to study radio journalism.

By this time, I'd worked acquired quite a lot of work experience with several local radio stations, so I basically breezed through the course and passed.

But just before the end of the course, I was warned not to expect to ever get a job in radio.

Three months after the course, I did actually get a job as a production assistant with one of London's major stations.

The opportunities to use the wide range of skills I'd acquired were immense and the future looked very bright.

Then I told my employers of my desire to be a

presenter, confident that I could do it and do it well.

They didn't share my confidence and kept telling me I couldn't do it.

Another station called Choice FM offered me a Sunday morning slot to host its new Gospel Show and my employers responded by drawing up a roster which required me to work on Sunday mornings.

My pleas for a change of working hours fell on deaf ears, no-one wanted to swap shifts with me and in the end, I had to take Sunday mornings off unpaid in order to be free to host the programme.

When my contract expired, the station decided I wasn't grateful enough to be working as a production assistant and on New Years Eve in 1990, they told me my services were no longer required.

Meanwhile over at Choice FM where I was hosting this Sunday Morning show, things were looking quite good, the programme was growing and attracting more of a following.

In 1992, I travelled to Atlanta where after two weeks of listening to a Gospel radio station everyday, my whole attitude to my programme changed.

I returned to London seeing my programme not just as a show but as a ministry and I began to treat it as such.

The listeners who up till that point had treated me as if I was the best thing since sliced bread now reacted as if I was the worst thing since the plague.

Before long, I'd become public enemy number one and my name drew derision and scorn everywhere I went.

By this time, my only source of income was this programme and I was living at home with my mother who was paying the rent where we lived.

She paid a year's rent in advance and left me in the house while she returned to Nigeria.

One night, a week after she left, there was a knock on the door and a man claiming to be the landlord told me he'd wondered why he hadn't received any rent for the last month.

It turned out the person whom we thought was the landlord was actually a tenant who'd hoped to get two months rent out of us.

Instead, he got a whole year's worth and had now conveniently disappeared.

In the next few months that followed, because the landlord wasn't prepared to go through the legal process, he resorted to all sorts of terror tactics to try to force me out of the house.

This included breaking into the house at will, cutting off the gas supplies and trying to disconnect the electricity.

My only way of keeping warm then was to take the fuses out every morning when I was leaving home and then put them back in when I came home at night.

I would lock myself in the bedroom with my clothes and trainers laid out in such a way that I was ready to throw them on and run if I needed to, in the event of any midnight visits.

Many people who heard this often wondered why I didn't just leave, but for me, the question was: where would I go?

Eventually in the New Year, I met a friend who offered me a room in his home and helped me with arranging housing benefits so the rent could be paid.

I had a roof over my head and finally re-discovered what it was like to have a peaceful and worry-free night's sleep again.

But with very little money, I struggled to make ends meet and frequently went without food for long periods.

At Choice FM, I procured the favour of my fellow presenters who would frequently send me out to buy their lunch and would also buy mine as my reward for making the trips for them.

Every now and again, I would be asked to host a concert on Saturday night and would be paid for it although I frequently had to chase the promoters around to get them to pay me afterwards.

Those were probably some of the most embarrassing Saturday evenings I experienced, as I often stood in front of halls full of people who didn't like me and made no secret of it.

And with no money for a decent outfit, I often stood in front of these people feeling ashamed because my clothes were in tatters and my shoes had holes in them, which were visible from the front.

This for me was poverty at its worst.

Things became no longer acceptable one Saturday evening.

In those days, I had no car and therefore had to

sleep at the station on Saturday nights so I could be ready to start my programme at six o clock on Sunday morning.

On this particular night, I lay there feeling desperately hungry and felt I couldn't go through the night without eating.

In desperation, I approached the presenter who was on-air and asked if he could lend me £5 to get some food.

He gave me the money, but he laughed in my face and asked; "Didn't your God provide for you?"

The shame was unbearable.

Yet I couldn't give him back the money because I was too hungry.

In my desperation and shame, I pleaded with God for a change of circumstances.

But, that was at least one occasion when I was able to say, I sought the Lord and He heard me and delivered me from all my fears.

In 1995, I joined Premier Radio.

Four years later in 1999, I married the lady of my dreams and have never looked back since.'

The moral in this story is that no matter how low you sink, as long as you refuse to give up on yourself, you will eventually come through.

Now read on and learn seven lessons Benny learnt from some of his most memorable experiences.

CHAPTER 1

PRINCIPLE 1: CHANGE STARTS FROM WITHIN

Romans 12 V. 2 ".....be transformed by the renewing of your mind...."

In 1995, Dr Creflo Dollar came to London for a series of meetings at what was then Glory Bible Church.

At the end of one of those meetings, I got to the doorway as I was making my way out of the church and came across a very beautiful woman standing there.

I was completely struck and after walking past her, I turned and just stood there for several minutes staring at her.

In the years that followed, I started to find out little bits about this woman and the more I learned, the more I liked her and wanted to get to know her better.

But at the same time, I never dared go anywhere near her because I didn't think I was good enough to be with someone like her.

Consequently, I sailed through the next few years' forming relationships with other women while knowing in the back of my mind that in the ideal world, this was the woman I would have wanted.

There was nothing wrong with any of the other women I ever dated, in fact they were all great and very special women of God that I probably did not even deserve to be with.

But I dated them because I felt that my ideal woman would never look at me, given all the other men around, whom I thought were more suitable for a woman of her calibre.

And after so many years of thinking I could never have the best of anything I wanted, I saw this lady as yet another example of what I could not have.

But today, that lady is my wife.

She became the first example in my life, that I was entitled to the best and could have it.

Before she agreed to marry me, she insisted she had to pray and hear from God first and I had a problem with that.

My fear was that if she prayed to God, He would never sanction her marrying me.

Despite all my protests and arguments and every ploy I tried to get her to fall in love with me, she stood her ground and wasn't swayed.

Much to my surprise, she got God's blessing and married me and for once in my life, I had the best.

Today, a great many people settle for much less than what God would dearly love to give them because of one problem: how they think.

So now I understand why Paul tells the Romans to be transformed by the renewing of their minds.

The lesson in there for you and I today is that the first key to changing our lives is changing the way we think.

Too often in today's society many of us delay the changes we want in our lives because we think that it's the circumstances outside us that need to change.

But if we are to move from wherc we are, the first thing we need is not a change of houses or a change of jobs or salary, or even a change of spouse.

The first change we need is in the arena of our minds.

God says if we are willing and obedient, we will enjoy the best of the land and that speaks to our attitudes, which again are formed by our thinking patterns.

He didn't say if we change cars or jobs or homes or spouses or anything else for that matter, we would have the best

If you want a change in your life, you must start to see yourself and see your current circumstances in a different light.

See yourself as a child of God, and a blessed one at that.

In Romans 8 vs. 16, the bible says God's Spirit bears witness with our spirit that we are children of God; this settles your identity.

You must not see your circumstances as problems, but see them as provokers that will make you a better person and push you towards your God-ordained destiny.

There is scriptural authority for thinking this way too.

In the Living Bible translation of James 1 vs. 2 - 3 we are told: " Dear brothers, is your life full of difficulties and temptations? Then be happy, for when the way is rough, your patience has a chance to grow. So let it grow, and don't try to squirm out of your problems. For when your patience is finally in full bloom, then you will be ready for anything, strong in character, full and complete"

So what you need now is not another handout or someone else's help, but a change in the way you think.

If your way of thinking doesn't change, all the money in the world may grant you temporary relief, but you'll soon be back to square one.

That's why so many people win millions of pounds on the lottery only to become poor very soon afterwards.

Money doesn't change you, it only makes you more of what you already are.

Instead of looking at your situation and thinking that this is as good as it gets, or that it's your fault for being where you are, begin to see yourself as God's child and see where you are as just a bus stop in the journey towards where you are going.

Contrary to what you may presently believe, this is NOT as good as it gets and even if it's your fault that you are where you are right now, it does not mean that you deserve the situation you are in.

"How do I change my thinking, Benny?" I hear you ask.

In order to change your thinking patterns, you will have to be more selective about whom and what has access to you, your eyes, your ears and your heart.

In Proverbs 4 v. 23, God says guard your heart with all diligence because it is the wellspring of life. (NIV)

To diligently guard you heart means being careful what you see and what you hear.

The things that you see and hear are the very things that determine how you think and how you think is what determines what you eventually become.

In order to ensure that we turn out as God had originally intended, we must begin to think in line with what God says about us in His Word.

You have the power to change your situation if you are not happy with it.

But that change - if it is to last - has got to begin in your mind.

"When your heart decides a destination, your mind will determine the map to help you get there."
Dr Mike Murdock

A change of circumstances will also require a change of focus.

One of the lowest points in Abraham's life had to have been when his nephew Lot left him, as noted in Genesis chapter 13.

Here was a young man who had become very wealthy as a result of his association with Abraham.

This new found wealth led to attitudes which caused disputes between Lot's and Abraham's herdsmen, this eventually forced both men to part ways.

Abraham had been responsible for his nephew's success and now this was all the thanks he was getting; the ingratitude must have been heart-wrenching!!!

But God's first words in Gen. 13 vs 14 were: "Lift up your eyes from where you are..."

If you and I are to change our circumstances, less time must be spent looking at and meditating on these circumstances and more time must be spent concentrating on where you want to be.

If you do not focus your mind on where you want to go, you won't be motivated enough to do anything to get there.

As Dr Mike Murdock once said during a meeting in London, "When your heart decides on a destination, your mind will design the route to get you there."

Instead of looking repeatedly at where you are and blaming yourself or throwing a pity party, start looking towards where you'd rather be.

The more attractive you find it, the more you'll want to get there, and the more you will want to get away from where you are.

One of my lifelong dreams has always been to fly planes.

The times I have wanted to do something about that dream have always been when I have watched videos of people flying jets and picturing myself doing the same thing.

It is a picture of where you want to be, firmly planted in your mind that will motivate you to move from where you are, right now.

If you cannot see it in your mind, you won't be motivated to do those things that will help you to eventually see it for real.

CHAPTER 2

PRINCIPLE 2:
GET TO KNOW AND LOVE YOURSELF

Matthew 19 vs. 19: "…Thou shalt love thy neighbour as thyself…."

One of the most frightening Summers of my life was that of 1978.

The worry began in Lagos, Nigeria, one morning at the start of July, when my parents as well as my brothers, my sister and I went to the British High Commission to get entry visas which would allow us to visit the United Kingdom.

At the time, the British High Commission had a fearsome reputation when it came to granting would-be visitors entry visas.

Rightly or wrongly, the general belief was that when you went there, your chances of getting a visa were slim to none.

I'm not so sure about my parents, but I know that we the children were very worried that our applications would be rejected.

We emerged very relieved at the end of the day with the coveted visas and three weeks later, at Murtala Muhammed International Airport, Lagos, I boarded a British Caledonian Airways flight bound for London.

After all the excitement of flying in a plane died down (it was only the third time I'd ever flown), I faced up to the reality of my trip and I spent the remainder of the flight filled with terror at the thought of what might be waiting for me in London.

You see, the official reason given for my visit was 'holiday', but tucked away inside my jacket pocket was an admission letter from a college in Oxford.

I was going to Britain to study, but had been warned over and over again about the dire consequences of this ever being known to the authorities once I got there.

And now, as the big blue D-C-10 jet powered through the night skies, with its golden lines glistening in the moonlight, all kinds of possibilities played through my mind, each with the same end : that somehow, the real reason for my trip would be discovered.

I made it through the immigration section at Gatwick Airport, heaving sighs of relief just about strong enough to blow the airport away and then a few weeks later, a new fear emerged.

What would happen when it was time to get my visa renewed?

Would the Home Office frown at the fact that I 'decided' to stay and study or would they think it had been a deception?

And what would happen if they decided not to renew the visa?

How would I cope with the shame and embarrassment of being sent back to Nigeria where I would have to face all my friends who thought I would be in London for much longer?

In fact, there was no need for any of these fears.

Right there in my passport, it was noted that I had been born in England.

I was a British citizen!!!

There had been no need for all the bother of going to the High Commission in Nigeria to get an entry visa because as a British citizen, I was entitled to live in Britain if I wanted to.

So at the appropriate time, my passport was sent to

the Home Office, they acknowledged that I was born in England and advised my mother and I to begin the short process that resulted in my obtaining a British passport.

All the worry, I had put myself through was all for nothing because of what I did not know.

The moral of all this is that the greatest loss we will ever suffer as believers is caused by the fact that too many of us do not know who we are, or who we are in Christ.

When you do not know who you are, you will also not know what your entitlements are and you will lose them immediately.

We are told in scripture that Satan's plan is to steal, kill and destroy.

With many believers, he doesn't need to steal because much of what he takes is surrendered to him by the believer with thanksgiving and praise, and in fact only eternity will ever reveal how many benefits we lost because we did not even know we were entitled to them.

The bible describes the devil as the prince of darkness; in the Hebrew language, 'darkness' is another word for ignorance and as such, Satan is a prince of darkness who rules by ignorance.

Satan gets his power from what you and I don't know, and especially what we don't know of our identity in Christ.

You cannot make a success of your life until you find out who you are in Christ and learn also to love who you are.

Because I did not know I was a British citizen, I did not know I was entitled to live in Britain and was seeking permission to go and remain there from people who had no more right to be in Britain than I did.

And let me say straightaway that the biggest mistake you could ever make in this life is to try to define yourself on the basis of what other people say.

The only source for finding out who you are MUST be the One who made you and who knows what He made : God, your eternal Father and Creator. So what is God's definition of who you are ?First in Genesis 1 vs. 26, we are told that God decided to make you and I in His image and according to His likeness.

This means that you and I are like God, and as a son has the attributes of his father, even so, you and I have His character, nature and attributes.

I am now going to list some of these attributes, but before I do that, I must first point out one attribute, which is a must, if the others are to emerge.

Isaiah 6 vs. 3 says He is holy and then in the New Testament in 2 Corinthians 5 vs 21 we are described as the righteousness of God in Christ.

It is not something we have to strive to be, we already ARE righteous.

I hasten to point this out from the onset because the absence of this attribute will rob us of our right to experience any of the others which I am about to highlight.

The first attribute you and I share with God, which I would like to highlight is the right to succeed.

In Genesis 1, we are told that everything that God did was good and in fact when it came to you and I, we are told He saw that we were 'very good'.

In Psalms 1, we are told, "whatsoever we do shall prosper".

This means that you have a right to enter into your endeavours expecting to succeed and it is important that you hold on to and constantly remind yourself of this, otherwise you will sometimes take on projects not expecting to succeed and you will simply fail.

Ephesians 1 verse 3 says God is blessed and it goes on to say you and I are blessed.

To be blessed means to be empowered to prosper or to succeed in whatever God has called us to do.

As a child of God, made in His own image and according to His likeness, you are born to succeed, not fail.

Genesis Chapter 1 depicts a God who made a decision and carried it through and who could not be stopped by anything.

Nowhere in that chapter or anywhere else in the bible are we told that there was anything that God set out to do which was frustrated by anything.

In Joshua 1 vs. 5, Joshua is given the same promise that accrues to you and I today.

"No-one will be able to stand up against you all the days of your life..." (NIV)

I considered it vital to use these two examples because there are too many believers around today, whose lives have ground to a halt because they tried something and it didn't succeed.

They gave up and they accepted as their lot in life, the failure that was never part of God's make-up or theirs.

In Romans 8, we are told that we are heirs of God and in case we begin to undermine this, we are also described as joint heirs with Christ, which means that everything Jesus has inherited from God is also available to us.

The key to succeeding in life then is to first find out who you are in Christ and base your discovery SOLELY on the basis of God's Word, not the opinions of people.

I will not say much at this point about people's opinions as that is the subject of a later chapter in this book.

Once you begin to find out who you are, you will find that when God made you, He did not leave the job unfinished.

He saw that you were very good.

You were the best when He made you and that has not changed.

He never made you to live a life that is a mess and if that is where you are now, you will be there only for as long as you decide to stay there.

Succeeding in life starts with knowing who you are and knowing that because of who you are, you deserve nothing less than the best.
It is also important to love the person you know yourself to be.

Jesus taught in the New Testament that we are to love our neighbour as ourselves; in other words, love your neighbour as much as you love yourself.

This means that if you do not love yourself, you cannot really love your neighbour.

Loving yourself begins with knowing that God, who is the source of all wisdom and knowledge and who knows your worst faults more than even you know them, actually loves you.

In Romans 5 vs. 8, we are told that God demonstrates His love towards us in that while we were still sinners, Christ died for us.

While we were still sinners!!!

Not after we did enough to deserve it, but while we were still sinners.

If God loves you despite everything He knows of you, then you have no business disliking yourself.
God told the Israelites in Deuteronomy 1 vs. 6

"...You have dwelt long enough in this mount; turn you and take your journey..." (King James Version)

For the purpose of this book, I came to alert you that you have been at this point in your life long enough.

A decision to turn now would represent a change of direction in terms of your thoughts about the situation you are facing right now.

It is time to recognise that you were not intended by God to make a destination out of your present location.

You are too important, you deserve better and there are too many people whose lives depend on you to moving forward, into what God has promised and proposed you.

We sometimes make it easier for ourselves to become comfortable with where we are because we think we are the only ones affected.

At the time of writing this book, I was facing enormous challenges and it would have been easy for me to become depressed and feel sorry for myself.

But I knew that a book like this was inside me and

I recognised that there are too many people who need the message in this book, so I could not afford to waste time indulging in a prolonged pity party.
Similarly, there are lives that will turn around for the better once you refuse to accept your present location and once you make a decision to strive for the wealthy place into which God wants to bring you.

God is not going to come and forcibly move you while you sit around doing nothing, He will help you once you make a decision to move, because you have realised that as a child of God, you deserve and are entitled to something better.

You have indeed dwelt at this mountain long enough, it is time for you to move on into your God-ordained wealthy place.

CHAPTER 3

PRINCIPLE 3: RECOGNISE THERE IS NO PROGRESS WITHOUT PURPOSE

Romans 8 vs. 28: "And we know that in all things, God works for the good of those who love Him, who have been called according to His purpose."

At 5am one bright summer morning in 1990, I stepped into the empty offices and studio complex of a radio station in south London.

The station was transmitting, but as it had no overnight presenters in those days, it was in automation and I was due to go live at six o clock.

It was to be my first ever live broadcast as a gospel music radio presenter and I was desperately nervous.

The show, when it began, was actually a breeze, give or take a few mistakes as I battled to get familiar with the mixer.

In the next two years that followed, I struggled to put together a show that sounded like the rest of the station and while I just about managed it, it was very hard work demanding big sacrifices for small rewards.

When I took over the programme, I was struck by the lack of interest within the Christian community, which was supposed to be its market.

It was broadcast between 6am and 8am on Sunday mornings, and most people said that this slot was too early and they couldn't be bothered to wake up and listen; they preferred to sleep instead.

And so I spent many Saturday nights up, in the studio, preparing programmes with this sinking feeling at the back of my mind, that the people for whom I was going through all this trouble were not even going to wake up and listen

Other gospel presenters, on stations where they had better time slots than mine, frequently and unashamedly laughed at me because of the time slot which I had.

The discouragement was beyond words.

Then in 1992, I travelled to the United States for two weeks and while I was there I began to listen everyday to a Mid-morning programme on what was then Atlanta's AM gospel music radio station 1380 WAOK.

By the time the two weeks were over, my whole perception of what I was doing on radio had changed and I knew I couldn't come back to London and just spin discs and play the smoothie Sunday morning radio personality.

At the same time, I met a man who was to become my spiritual father and mentor Dr Myles Munroe through whom I came in contact - for the first time - with the concept of Purpose.

As I meditated more on this word, I realised that my life could not continue to be just a day-to-day experience.

I was born and I was on radio for a purpose and that purpose had to govern everything I did.

The more I discovered the purpose for my radio programme, the more I realised it was a ministry that had to be properly planned and executed.
I couldn't just go on radio and play songs because they were good, they all had to fit in with the general and specific purpose of each programme.

At that point, I recognised that in a radio fraternity, where all the other gospel music presenters on other stations said they were trying to use their programmes to win souls for Christ, I was called to keep for Christ the souls, which everyone was winning.

That meant my show had to consist of a lot of songs, scriptures and spoken messages from guest preachers all addressing the challenges that frequently forced many Christians to backslide and depart from their faith in God.

Once I caught that revelation, the programme zapped forward like a rocket.
What started out as a two-hour programme soon became a thriving 4-hour extravaganza, three hours of which were syndicated to another station in Birmingham, something no other gospel presenter anywhere else in the country had.

But what gave me the greatest satisfaction was knowing that all the other gospel radio presenters who had laughed at me in the beginning, were now all approaching the station asking for me to be taken off the programme, because they felt they could do a better job.
None of them remembered all the Saturday nights when they were all in their beds sleeping, while I was at the studio preparing a two-hour programme which they didn't think anyone would want to hear.

I took the same concept of purpose to Premier Radio where what started as a two-hour programme soon became of four hours duration and in 1997, it became a part of the station's daily programme schedule.

Again after I left my Sunday morning show, the general consensus was that I was finished.

I was leaving the biggest gospel programme in Britain to take over a two-hour unknown Saturday evening show on an AM station, which hardly anyone ever listened to.

What they said back then was that no one would be in to listen to my programme because it was transmitted on Saturday evening when most of the people who had an interest in gospel music would be out at concerts and other church events.
In addition, there was the general belief that even those who were home would never want to listen to the radio on Saturday night when television presented a much better alternative; not to mention the fact that no-one would be able to find the station as everyone only listened to FM stations and no-one supposedly knew where the AM band was.

But having decided that moving to Premier was God's will for me, I knew there had to be a purpose for my being there and as long as I committed myself to that purpose, I would be okay.

I set about fulfilling that purpose which was to edify the Christian and gospel community and once again, success followed.

First I was awarded another slot, which was a Sunday evening in addition to my Saturday slot.

And then a few months later, I became the first gospel music radio presenter in Britain to be employed full-time hosting gospel programmes.

The moral in this little trip down memory lane is that if you find you are stuck in a rut today with your life seemingly going nowhere, and then perhaps like I did, you need to grasp the whole concept of Purpose.

You were not born simply because your mummy and daddy came together in a blaze of passion one night under the starry skies and decided to have you.

In fact, long before each of your parents even knew the other existed, you were already on God's mind; He planned for you to be born and He chose the place and time of your birth.

'But Benny, my parents told me I wasn't planned.' I hear you reply.

That makes your existence even more important.

It simply means that your birth was so important that God had to override your parents' plans to get you here.

Understanding that reason why God wanted you here and applying yourself fully to it is the key to getting yourself out of the rut you may be in right now.

The same also applies to your re-birth as a Christian.

Too many people cheat themselves out of their birthright as God's children by thinking that they were born again just so that after they die, or when the rapture happens, they can go to heaven.
Nothing could be further from the truth.

Your place in heaven is a side effect of your salvation, it was not the original purpose.

God had a plan for your life when you were born, but falling into sin made that plan impossible to carry out.

As such, God had to send His only begotten Son to die for your sins so that you could be born again and be fit to fulfil the original purpose for which you were created.

To begin to understand the purpose for your birth, let us look at some words contained in our Lord's Prayer.
The third and fourth lines in that prayer say "Thy kingdom come. Thy will be done on earth as it is, in heaven."

The term 'Kingdom' here does not refer to a place; it refers to God's kingly dominion.

It is simply God's way of doing things.
That prayer expresses God's desire for His kingdom to be manifest here on earth; in other words, for things to be done here on earth God's way, as well as for His will to come to pass on earth like it does in heaven.

With this in mind, Jesus says in Matthew 6 vs. 33 that you and I are to seek first God's kingdom and His righteousness and then all the other things we want out of this life will be added to us.

You have a part to play towards the establishment of God's kingly dominion here on earth, in your neighbourhood and in your place of work.

For this, you have been given gifts and abilities, which are the equipment for doing the job.

So Jesus is saying in Matthew 6 vs. 33 that when you play your part in making His kingdom come and causing His will to be done on earth, you will find yourself in a position where the things you have spent so much of your time pursuing will now begin to pursue you.

Your part in advancing God's will and kingdom on earth is also closely linked to your passions and

the things you enjoy doing.
If God comes right now and gives you a pen and a piece of paper and then asked you to write a list of the things you would most dearly like to do, with a promise that whatever was on that list would happen, what would you write ?

If you had the chance to do it, what would you be willing to do, without any pay?

These are two vital keys to understanding your purpose.

Many of us go through life treating as hobbies, the things that God meant for us to earn our living from.

I am passionate about radio and spent many years doing it for free as a pirate broadcaster.

At one stage, I drove more than 100 miles every Sunday evening to host a programme on radio with no pay, I just loved it.

Now, I enjoy the unbelievably fulfilling pleasure of doing what I love and getting paid very well for doing it.

I cannot tell you how many times I have leapt out of my bed in the morning because I had a great and exciting idea of something that I wanted to do on my radio programmes, and just couldn't wait to get it done.

You too can enjoy that same pleasure and you will, once you discover your purpose.

Discovering your purpose will immediately begin to rule out things and people that will not help you to get that purpose fulfilled.
It will also begin to help you to determine exactly where you should be, what jobs you should be doing and who you should be associating with.

During those days when I was driving hundreds of miles just to do a radio programme, it was knowing my destination that helped me to decide which routes to take and which motorways I did not need to be driving towards.

Your purpose will also put guidelines in your life that will save you a lot of time, expense and frustration.

If you do not feel at the moment as if your life is going anywhere, what you need is not another job or a move to a new house or even a change of spouse.

What you need now is a discovery or re-discovery of your purpose; once that is settled, your progress will be unstoppable.

Another thing your purpose will do is it will help you to put certain other things into their proper perspective and I think it is important for me to make this point for the sake of people who lose their joy over the way other people treat them.

When the purpose of something is not known, its abuse becomes inevitable.

When people mistreat you, you are NOT the problem, they are.

There is nothing wrong with you, the problem is their perception of you.

It is the fact that they do not know their own purpose, never mind yours that is causing them to abuse you.

Purpose protects you from abusing your own life and it protects you from the bad feelings that come with other people trying to abuse you.

I will finish this chapter with a reference to a recorded quote from Dr Myles Munroe, which I frequently play on my radio programme.

"The greatest tragedy in life is not death, but life without purpose."

CHAPTER 4

PRINCIPLE 4 - BE WILLING TO BE DIFFERENT

Daniel 1 vs. 8 : "But Daniel purposed in his heart that he would not defile himself with the portion of the king's meat, nor with the wine which he drank: therefore he requested of the prince of the eunuchs that he might not defile hi drank: therefore he requested of the prince of the eunuchs that he might not defile he might not defile himself."

In the early 90s, a gospel music artiste released a song, which turned out to be very popular.

Such was its acclaim that even the secular radio presenters played it on their programmes and it managed to achieve the crossover into mainstream radio.

In those days, requests and dedications were very much a part of my radio programme.

These, along with what's on columns giving out free publicity for events on the Christian calendar, were very much the norm in gospel music radio.

So, naturally, when I announced that it was time for people to call in to request their favourites, I was always inundated with requests for this particular song.

But one day, as I sat listening to the song in question, I suddenly realised that even though it had a very beautiful melody and beat, its lyrics were not in agreement with scripture.

It sounded right, it sounded Christian, it was in fact a prayer, but it contradicted every biblical teaching on prayer.

So in one morning, I became public enemy number one with three announcements.

First, I was never going to play that song on the programme again, second, I was not going to do requests anymore and third, if anyone wanted publicity for their events on my programme, they had to pay for commercial spots like everyone else.

My reasoning was that if a song contradicted scripture, it had no place on a Christian programme.

And requests, on a programme, which was a ministry, were like a preacher stepping into the pulpit and asking his congregation to pick their favourite sermons, which he would then preach. I further argued that if churches could not afford to pay for commercial advertising on the radio, I wasn't helping them by giving them free publicity; instead what I was doing was catering for their poverty.

No other gospel music radio presenter was taking this stand so it served only to isolate me further, but my mind was made up and there was no going back.

In the months that followed, everyone who could string two words together criticised me through telephone calls, letters and attacks to my face when people saw me at social events.

At its worst, one member of the gospel community invited me to lunch and then spent two hours telling me about all the negative things people were saying about me and the programme and what he thought I could do to clean up my image.

Here was a Christian telling me about a gospel music radio programme, but who had given no consideration to what God wanted; his sole concern was what people were saying.

So now, I was supposed to go and change my programme, based on the comments of people whom I didn't know and who clearly felt more comfortable speaking to him rather than me.

But then towards the end of the year, as I made a decision to stick to the new path I'd chosen, things began to look up.

First the ratings which had gone down now tripled and soon, the Gospel programme was in the station's top three in terms of ratings.

By the time I left, it was joint top of the ratings and as I applied the same principle of doing something different, I began to experience different things too, culminating in my eventually becoming the only gospel music radio presenter who was doing it full-time.

The price for this was a decision to be a Daniel and refusal to follow the crowd.

Friend, there is nothing wrong with you as God made you and the biggest mistake you could make in life is to try to please or be like everybody else.

In fact, in the New Living translation of Isaiah 43 vs. 4, God says "….you are precious to me, you are honoured and I love you…."

That is a declaration of love that God makes to you just the way you are.

Stepping out to be the 'You' that God loves unconditionally means being different from everyone else, and you must be prepared for the criticism and unpopularity that this will bring to you.

Joseph's troubles began when he announced his dreams and they were different to the mediocrity which his brothers had decided they would accept for the rest of their lives.

Daniel's descent down the slippery slope into the lion's den began when he made a decision not to be like all the other governors; and his colleagues Shadrach, Meschach and Abednego started their journey into the fiery furnace as soon as they too chose not to follow the crowd.

But once they all decided to stick to their guns look what happened.

Joseph became the Prime Minister of Egypt, while Daniel, Shadrach, Meschach and Abednego were all promoted above their critics and accusers in Babylon.

In fact, in Daniel's case, his accusers ended up in the same den where the lions which had not been hungry when he was in there, suddenly rediscovered their appetite.

You do not owe anyone any apologies for being the way you are.

For sure, there is always room for improvement in each one of us, but this does not involve living up to the expectations of everyone else and trying to be something or someone you are not.

Being all that God has created you to be will involve being totally different from what everybody expects you to be and not everyone is going to like you for that.

But as long as you are faithful and stay true to yourself, then ultimately you will come out on top, which is where God wants you to be.

Being yourself will enable you to live a life that sends out a powerful message to the rest of the world about God's goodness.
And as you stick to being your original self, your critics will eventually recognise the error of their ways.

This is why God promises in the Amplified version of Isaiah 54 vs. 17 that "..every tongue that rises against you in judgement you will show to be in the wrong…."(Amplified Version)

When God wanted plants and animals, He spoke to the earth.

When He wanted fishes, He spoke to the sea and when He wanted to create you, He spoke to Himself and you came out of Him.

He didn't get it wrong or make a mistake, you were exactly what He wanted and He didn't check with any of your critics first to see whether you were okay.

The bible tells us that after He finished creating you, He saw that you were VERY GOOD.

Once you start trying to be like other people, you become something different from the 'very good' which God created.

Today, the source of your discouragement may stem from the fact that after you started trying to be yourself and were prepared to be different, the whole world turned against you.

But I want you to know that even if the whole world was against you, those that are for you are still more and greater.

Stand your ground, don't back down and don't try to conform.

People who do not like you because you refuse to be the same as everybody else are really just resentful because you have taken a step, which they did not have the courage to take.

They see that you are stepping out of the realm of average to be the special person that God created you to be and they don't like it because when you become different, you highlight their mediocrity.

There are more than six billion people on the earth today and not one of them has your genetics or even you fingerprints, because you were not called to be like anyone else.

Celebrate your differences; it is the key to reaching the above average destiny that God has in store for you.

In the end, you can either be popular or powerful but you cannot be both.

CHAPTER 5

PRINCIPLE 5: IGNORE THE EXPERTS

John 11 vs. 39: "Jesus said, Take ye away the stone. Martha, the sister of him that was dead, saith unto Him, Lord, by this time he stinketh: for he hath been dead four days."

In 1988, having concluded that I was called to be in radio, I decided to take a one-year course leading to the award of a Certificate in Radio Journalism.

Just weeks before the course was due to finish, my tutor invited a few of us out for a drink with him one Friday afternoon.

Then the bomb dropped.

After he'd had enough whisky and lager inside him to loosen his tongue sufficiently, he said to me as calmly as you like: "Ben, you will never get a job in radio."

The statement was bad enough on its own, but to hear it in front of other members of the course was devastating as well as embarrassing.

I had left my family in the West Midlands and travelled to London to take the course and it had been an awful wrench to spend all that time away from them.

Now, just as I was starting to look forward to the reward, which would make the sacrifice worthwhile, here was this man telling me that in effect, it had all been a waste of my time.
He should have known too.

Before taking up lecturing, he'd been a news editor working on both television and radio.

This man had hired and worked with a great many journalists; he was well experienced and could easily be regarded as an expert in the business, and the kind whose opinions you ignored at your peril.

His reasoning was that being of African origin I had a strong and audible accent, which would be a turn-off for listeners.

Basically, what he was saying was that the British people, so used to hearing the Queens English and other more acceptable accents of British origin, would never tolerate an African accent, which meant no radio employer would want to hire me.

I am not sure he realised what level of bigotry he attributing to the people of the country.

In a state of panic after hearing this bombshell, I was ready to do just about anything to avoid having wasted a whole year at college, on a course which I was now being told would do nothing to enhance my chances of securing employment.

So, in the weeks that followed, I stayed behind after lectures everyday, to take news reading lessons all geared towards helping me to lose my accent.

The recommendation was that as other television newsreaders of minority ethnic origin had done it, I could do it too.

After a while, I rebelled and stopped the extra lessons, having decided that I could never sound British, and didn't wish to.

I reminded the tutor that I was going into radio because I felt that it was God's purpose for my life and that if it was indeed God-ordained, then He would make a way for me to get in, accent or not.

Within three months of finishing the course and passing, I got my first job with a radio station in London as a production assistant.

By the time I was through my first year, I'd started wanting more than just answering phones on someone else's programme; I wanted my own programme.

I expressed this desire to my employers who'd had many more years of broadcasting experience than I had and who were therefore experts in the industry.

They had worked with the best radio presenters in the business and none of them thought I was good enough.

Shortly afterwards, another station offered me a slot on Sunday mornings to host a Gospel music programme and that was the beginning of my ministry in this field.

My full-time employers didn't like it and it wasn't long before their spite surfaced.

The senior producer drew up a new roster for production assistants and under this new roster; I was scheduled to work on Sunday mornings.

To get out of this, I volunteered to take Sunday mornings off unpaid, which they agreed, but eventually, when my 18-month employment contract ended, they decided that I wasn't grateful enough being a production assistant and I was duly fired.

My Sunday morning programme on the other station thrived - complete with my accent which I'd been told no-one would ever tolerate - and eventually, I joined another station where they subsequently paid me to do the programme full-time.

Sadly, the man who told me I'd never get a job in radio died before he could see how wrong he was.

Only eternity will ever truly reveal how many people's destiny of greatness was sacrificed on the altar of someone else's opinion.

Indeed it is your ability to pursue your dreams regardless of what people think about all the odds stacked against you that will mark you out for greatness.

A couple of examples will help to illustrate this point.

Walt Disney was fired from his first job with a newspaper because the editor didn't think he was creative enough.

F. W. Woolworth was not allowed any contact with customers at the store where he worked because his employers thought he was too stupid.

But both men rode the tide of 'experts' opinions and went on to make their mark and today, who can imagine a cartoon world without Walt Disney or a High Street anywhere in Britain without a

Woolworth's store?

Neither of these two people was any more gifted or better than you are.

You have a destiny of greatness just like they had and you too can make it regardless what other people - whom you would expect to know what they were talking about - have said.

The key to surviving the gauntlet of opinions - and especially those of the so-called experts - is knowing that the dream you are pursuing is one that has been given to you by God.

One way to identify this is when the dream itself is bigger than you and well beyond anything you can achieve in your own strength, making you totally reliant on God to bring it to pass, which means that He gets the glory out of your success.

When your vision and goals are God-ordained, you will be surrendering your passport to success if you give up because someone didn't think you could make it.

You must remember that the devil does not want you to succeed with your vision and he will do anything, or use anyone available, to dissuade you from pursuing it.

He wins when you decide to give up.

The experts are right about the impossibility of your vision, if you are choosing to be totally dependent on your own strengths.

When you choose to pursue that dream and trust God for it to come to pass, then you avail yourself of the unlimited power of a God for whom nothing is impossible.

Indeed His Son promises that if you have faith the size of a mustard seed, nothing will be impossible for you.

This is because you are made in the image of God and according to His likeness.

In other words, you are like Him.

If nothing is impossible with Him, then nothing is impossible for you, as long as it is within His purpose and will for your life.

So today, I come to encourage you to resurrect that dream that has been wrapped up for so long in the grave cloth of expert opinion and buried in the tomb of discouragement.

The bible says that the eyes of God are going to and fro across the earth, as He searches for someone on whose behalf He can show Himself strong.

If you have been told that your dream is impossible, then you have just qualified to experience the miracle-working power of God in your life.

God is now ready to show Himself strong on your behalf.

The discouraging opinions you have heard are merely the raw materials for the manifestation of God's power in your life; without these opinions, you would not have a story to tell someday.

As you rise above expert opinions and succeed where everyone thought you would fail, you will one day be able to use your experiences to encourage others not to give up on their dreams in the way that you did not give up on yours.

From here on in, every time you hear an expert telling you that what you want to achieve is not possible, or has never been done before, cancel that lie out of your mind with the truth of the following statement from God's Word.

Romans 3 vs. 4: "Let God be true and every man a liar."

CHAPTER 6

PRINCIPLE 6 - RECOGNISE THE PLUS AT YOUR CROSS

James 1 vs. 2 - 4 : "Consider it pure joy, my brothers, when you face trials of many kinds, because you know that the testing of your faith develops perseverance.
Perseverance must finish its work so that you may be mature and complete, not lacking anything."
(NIV)

I had often heard my pastor the Rev Matthew Ashimolowo say that "….miracles are born in the womb of adversity…." but it was not until the Summer of 1999 that I was to suddenly - and involuntarily - have my own experience of the truth of this statement.

After having been on the radio consistently - never off for more than two weeks at a time - since 1990, I was suddenly pulled off-air for three months.

Since I started hosting gospel music radio programmes, I always had a vision to host a programme, which would be syndicated throughout the United Kingdom and indeed throughout Africa, the Caribbean and the United States.

In 1999, I was approached by a Christian radio station in Uganda who now wanted me to send them recordings of my programme for transmission on a weekly basis.

The idea never got off the ground, but it served as the catalyst for me to do something about making my vision a reality, starting in Africa.

I quickly got three stations in Africa to start taking the programme, but what I was sending them was edited versions of what I'd been doing on my current job.

Only, my employers didn't know this and when they found out and asked me about it, I denied it at first and then eventually owned up to what I'd been doing.

The punishment was swift and hard.

First, I was suspended without pay for two weeks while they decided whether I would continue working for them.

After the two weeks passed, I was brought in to be told I would be off-air for three months and was being demoted to the position of a production assistant during that time.

My salary was also ten thousand pounds less than

what I'd been paid as a presenter.

With a wedding due to take place in Nigeria three months later and nothing paid for except a deposit on flights to Lagos for my fiancée and I, a cut in wages was the last thing I needed.

The advice I got at the time was quite sensible: delay the wedding until you know what is going to happen to you.

But I remembered a message preached by Dr Mike Murdock in which he said one reason why people never experienced God's miracle-working power in their lives was their unwillingness to ever place themselves in a position where a miracle was needed.

With this in mind and drawing on what my pastor had said about miracles in the womb of adversity, I told my fiancée that the wedding was going ahead as planned.

Ellie Ewing, a character in the American television soap opera "Dallas" once said that a man's wealth is not measured by his money or power, but by his friends and I was about to find out just how true this statement was.

In the end, the only thing I paid for was my wedding ring as well as engagement and wedding rings for my fiancée and this was because I insisted that no man was going to pay for the rings on my wife's fingers.

Apart from that, everything else was paid for by my friends who all rallied round and allowed themselves to be used by God to be such a blessing at a time when I needed one.

Our flights to Nigeria, the wedding reception, complete with the food, the hall and decorations, the hotel accommodation for our wedding night, the flights and hotel accommodation for our honeymoon and everything else we needed for the wedding was all taken care of.

The strange thing was that when I was on a full salary, we never seemed able to pay for anything towards the wedding, but now my salary was a whole lot less, everything was paid for within a couple of weeks.

Time and time again on my programme, I had told my listeners about how God would supply all our need according to His riches in glory by Christ Jesus, and now, I had become a living witness as to how true this statement was.

But it took this terrible adversity for me to be able to come to knowledge of this truth.

Too often as believers, we go through adversities, which we have to experience over and over again because we fail to see the opportunities, which each trial brings with it.
It would have been all too easy for me to focus on the humiliation of being suspended and having to work in a demoted capacity alongside my other colleagues who knew what was going on.

It would have been easy to focus on the inconvenience of losing almost half my wages for three months.

But I think that if I had chosen to go down this path, I would have missed the opportunity to learn that God - not my employers - was my source.

The first thing many of us do when adversity hits us is to engage in all the feelings of sadness, depression and discouragement arising out of what has happened.

But today, I've come to remind you that however big the challenge you are facing right now may be, there is an even bigger God right behind it.
We must recognise that whatever trials come our way, we may have been helpless to stop them but God is not helpless.

He could have prevented the trials from ever manifesting if He wanted to.

If He chose to let it happen, it's because He was giving us an opportunity to experience the story before the manifestation of His glory.

You cannot know God as a provider until you are in lack.

You cannot know God as a healer until you are ill.

You cannot know God as the One who fights for you until you are under attack.

I think that after discovering your identity in Christ, one of the greatest keys to turning your trials into triumphs lies in your ability to see the opportunities, which those trials present you.

So now, instead of thinking about just how bad the challenge you are facing right now is, begin to look out for the opportunity, which it presents you.

Tomorrow, next week , next month, next year or even in two, three, five or even ten years from now, someone somewhere is going to face what you are going through right now.

It is your story about how you spotted the opportunity for a miracle in the midst of your challenge that will help to change that person's perspective and send them on their way to experiencing a miracle.

But you won't see that opportunity as long as you are focussed on the enormity of the challenge facing you.

Going back to scriptural examples will further help us to illustrate this point.

David did not rise from obscurity in the backwoods of Bethlehem until Goliath showed up defying Israel.

Joseph did not become the Prime Minister of Egypt until he was sold into slavery, falsely accused and imprisoned.

And the supreme example, our Lord Jesus Christ sits today at the right hand of God, but that didn't happen until He'd first been nailed to the cross.

The formula hasn't changed in your case.

The cross you face now is the plus that constitutes your passport to a personal experience of God's power and glory in your life.

And as we know about the likes of David and Joseph because of the challenges they faced, even so, in many years from now, people somewhere will know about you as a result of your victory over the challenge you face now.

That challenge is what will help to establish your identity as the winner that God created you to be.

I will finish this chapter with a reminder from Paul in the eighth chapter of his letter to the Romans.

"For your sake, we face death all day long; we are considered as sheep to be slaughtered.
No, in all these things we are more than conquerors through him who loved us."
NIV

In other words, outside (or without) these things, we are not more than conquerors. You cannot be a conqueror until you have conquered something and the cross you face right now is your opportunity to experience the victory that will establish your identity as a conqueror through Jesus Christ.

CHAPTER 7

PRINCIPLE 7: CULTIVATE TOTAL OBEDIENCE

Deuteronomy 28 vs. 2: "And all these blessings shall come upon you and overtake you, because you obey the voice your God" (NKJV)

I was in church for the weekly bible study one Friday night and as the pastor wound up his message and started to take up the offering, I suddenly found myself facing a dilemma.

At that time, I was still unemployed and all I was living on was the Income Support I was getting from my local authority as well as £20 per week, which I was being paid for my Sunday Morning Gospel Show on radio.

It was nowhere near enough to make ends meet.

Now on this Friday night, I was down to my last £3.48p, I had a car at home with an empty fuel tank and I still had to get to the studio the following Sunday morning to do my radio show.

On top of that, there was no food at home.

With pay day still about two to three weeks away,

there was no hope of any money coming in soon.

As the offering was being taken, a furious debate broke out in my mind as to exactly what I could afford to give.

First I thought about giving £1.48p and using the remaining £2 for petrol to get to the studio on the Sunday morning.

But then I felt that out of what I had, I had a duty to give God the lion's share which meant giving the £2 and keeping the remaining £1.48.

Then there was the added option of simply not giving anything, which I thought would have been reasonable in the circumstances, but I quickly ruled that out.

As the offering basket reached me, I got what I believed was the divine instruction and it was simple: "Give it all."

Before I had the time to remind God about the absurdity of this instruction, I threw the entire amount in my hand into the basket.

I then said; "Lord, I am now totally dependent on You, You know what my needs are for this weekend, so please deliver."

As I stepped out of the church, someone came up to me and asked to take a look at my bible.

They returned it to me later with an envelope in it, which I was told I could not open until I got home.

After getting home and praying, I opened the bible, took out the envelope and opened it to find £50 in it.

For many people, that would probably have been small change, but for me, it was like I'd won the National Lottery twice over!!!

I called the next day and couldn't stop saying "Thank You !!!". With tears streaming down my face at the generosity I had just benefited from.

Now, I thought to myself, I could get some food and put a decent amount of fuel in the car to get me to the studio on Sunday morning as well as to church afterwards.

Little did I realise that God was not finished with me.

Later that morning, a friend of mine invited me to her place for lunch.

She lived a long way from me and quite frankly, I was very reluctant to make the trip but she persisted and so I went.

After lunch, she invited me down to where her car was and she opened the boot, which was full of food and other necessaries and told me it was all mine.

She then drove with me down to the nearby petrol station where she paid to have my petrol tank filled before sending me on my way home.

So by Saturday evening, 24 hours after I'd given my last £3.48p, here I was, with a kitchen full of food, a car tank full of petrol and money in my pocket.

"Nothing pleases God more than our obedience and nothing hurts Him more than our disobedience."
Dr Mike Murdock

The gospel artiste Candi Staton says in one of her songs that "The greatest worship I can give is my obedience...."

Nothing demonstrates our trust and faith in God more than when we obey Him unquestioningly, even where what He is telling us to do may not quite make sense.

With no food at home and no petrol in the car, giving my last £3.48p as offering was probably not the most sensible or logical thing I could have done.

And had I explained it to anyone sitting near me, I am sure they would have understood perfectly if in the circumstances, I had chosen to hold on to what I had, rather than give it all.

In your present circumstances, you may feel that God is telling you to do something, which everyone else would probably call stupid.

You must realise though that ridiculous as it may seem, that step you are being asked to take may be the key to turning your circumstances around for good.

Bishop T. D. Jakes tells of how he spent his last $15,000 to print 5,000 copies of his first book 'Woman Thou Art Loosed'.

With his responsibilities as a family man, it would probably have been absurd of him to invest all that money on a book with no guarantees that it would sell.

Not only did it sell, it sold out in two weeks and he never looked back after that.

In 1995, when I had the option to leave Choice FM, having been unemployed for four years, no one thought it made sense for me to leave.

I was leaving a station where I had the biggest gospel radio programme in the United Kingdom.
I was leaving a thriving Sunday morning programme on an FM station for a new Saturday evening programme on an AM station, which hardly anyone listened to, in those days.

All I knew was that in the face of all the logical and sensible advice to stay which I was being given, I had a peace in my spirit that told me that God wanted me to move on.

Two years later, it became the full-time job I had not had for so long.

'Because you have rejected the word of the Lord, He has rejected you as king.'

When God decided to create man, He said "Let us make man in our image, in our likeness and let them rule…"

God rules over all things and as you and I were made in His image and according to His likeness, which means we are like Him, then we are also intended to rule in the way that He does.

The circumstances in which you find yourself today were never intended to control and rule over you, rather it was YOU who was supposed to rule over and dominate them.

You are supposed to rule because, having been made in God's image, you are a king in the way that He is.

That is why after He decided to make man in His own image, He added; "…let them rule…."(Gen. 1 vs. 26)

When you choose to walk in disobedience, that decision has the effect of stripping you of your mandate to rule over circumstances that present themselves before you.

In Deuteronomy 28 vs. 13, God promises;

"And the Lord will make you the head and not the tail; you will be above only, and not beneath, if you heed the commandments of the Lord your God, which I command you today, and are careful to observe them."
(NKJV)

So once again, we see that our ability to prevail over circumstances is directly linked to our ability to walk in obedience.
In challenging situations, the temptation to do what seems logical and right can prove extremely difficult to resist.

In the book of Proverbs 14 vs. 12, we are told; *"There is a way that seems right to man, but its end is the way of death"*

And while we may feel able to dismiss the biblical examples of people who benefited from their obedience, the example of Bishop TD Jakes makes it clear that obedience is the key to experiencing a divine turnaround.

What you see right now may make it imperative that you do something other than what God is telling you to do, but it is at a time such as this that you must remember that as a believer, you are called to walk by faith and not by what you see.

If a bible were to be written today, it is your ability to walk in obedience that will expose you to the miracles, which would mark you out for inclusion in its chapters.

God loves you.

In Jeremiah 29 vs. 11, God makes it clear that his thoughts towards you are of peace and not of evil; His desire is to give you a future and a hope.

He is never going to ask you to do anything that will lead to your harm.

Today then, as you ponder over what to do in the face of your present circumstances (which are only temporary and will pass anyway), ask yourself what miracles you could be cutting yourself off from, if you choose not to do what God is telling you to do.

"And you shall remember that the Lord your God led you all the way these forty years in the wilderness, to test you, to know what was in your heart, whether you would keep His commandments or not.
So He humbled you, allowed you to hunger, and fed you with manna which you did not know nor did your fathers know, that He might make you know that man shall not live by bread alone; but man lives by every word that proceeds from the mouth of God."
(Deuteronomy 8 vs. 2 - 3)

There are bigger and better breakthroughs waiting for you after the present set of challenges has passed.

There are blessings that God is waiting to bring into your life and in the face of those blessings, you will also be tempted to do things that are outside of God's will.

If you are able to obey Him unconditionally now, difficult though it may be, it will be easier to obey him later in easier circumstances.
Your ability to obey God today is what will qualify you for His blessings tomorrow.

CONCLUSION

"My brethren, count it all joy when you fall into diverse trials...."
- James 1 vs. 2

When adversities occur, it is easy in our human understanding to begin to rationalise and come up with logical reasons why we are going through such challenges.

The object of this book is not to absolve you of any responsibility for your own actions.

But at the same time, we must understand that even when we are at fault, God is still able to turn our mistakes into opportunities for the experience of His goodness and His power.

Every time the Israelites did evil in God's sight, they ended up in trouble and as they called upon the name of the Lord, the mistakes they made became opportunities to experience His saving power.

He would have been well within His rights to remind them that it was their sin that got them into their predicament.

He could easily have said; "You made your bed, now lie on it."

You and I would almost certainly say that, if we were in His shoes.

But in Romans 10 vs. 13 we are told; *"For whoever calls on the name of the Lord shall be saved."*

This means that even where we are the ones who have done what has caused the adversities we are facing, we can still call on Him and in so doing, position ourselves to see a manifestation of His power and glory in our lives.

Regardless the magnitude of the situation you are facing right now, there is one thing you can be sure about and it is this: **YOU CAN MAKE IT**.

Thrive, Don't Just Survive.

1 Corinthians 10 vs. 13 says that the challenge you face is not uncommon and God is faithful enough not to let you go through any more than you are able to deal with and He also promises that with your current circumstances, there is a way of escape.

This means that if you are facing these challenges, you can beat them, otherwise God would not let you go through them.

The biggest mistake you could make right now is to allow the devil to deceive you into thinking that your present challenges are bigger than anything you could cope with.

Everything you need in order to overcome is already inside you, none of it is in the hands of anyone else, because God loves you too much to set you up to be dependent on someone else.

Now, PLEASE understand that God's plan is NOT simply that you survive the present set of challenges you are up against.

Every challenge you face has been allowed by God to prepare you to move on from where you are now to some place bigger and better than where you were before the challenges showed up.

To make the most of our challenges, we must see them as something like the examinations which we all had to take at school before being promoted to the next class.

And the thing about God's school is that you never run out of chances to take the exams.

As long as you keep failing, He keeps letting you retake them.

You do not need to fail this time round, nor does God want you to fail.

An angel may not have come down from heaven to tell you this, but God ordained this book to be written as His way of letting you know He wants you to succeed.

"We are more than Conquerors through Him who loved us"

Not only does He want you to succeed, He wants you to finish up in a better place than where you are, right now.

Whether or not you get to that place depends entirely on you and how you want to come out of this present situation.

Before making that decision, please remember what God says about you in Romans 8 vs. 37.

In your present set of challenges, you are more than a conqueror; He didn't say you are more than a coper,

When these challenges have passed, your identity as more than a conqueror would have been firmly established.

Then like David, you too will be able to say; "It was good for me that I was afflicted."

I will finish this book with a quote from a song by an album by Bishop T.D. Jakes and the Potters House Mass Choir.

"This test is your storm, but it won't be long, go through, hold on"

HAPPY CONQUERING !!!